The Curve of Nature

Other poetry by Helen S. McCloskey

THE STRAIN OF ROOTS copyright @2003 by Helen S. McCloskey
Library of Congress Control Number 20033094314
Published by The Stinehour Press, Lunenburg, Vermont

The Curve of Nature

VERSE WRITTEN IN AND ABOUT OLD AGE

BY

Helen S. McCloskey

authorHOUSE®

AuthorHouse™
1663 Liberty Drive
Bloomington, IN 47403
www.authorhouse.com
Phone: 1-800-839-8640

Published by AuthorHouse 10/31/2013

ISBN: 978-1-4918-2299-9 (sc)
ISBN: 978-1-4918-2298-2 (hc)
ISBN: 978-1-4918-2297-5 (e)

Library of Congress Control Number: 2013917915

Cover Artwork by Marni Sinclair

This book is printed on acid-free paper.

I dedicate this small contribution to the family shelf

TO MY DAUGHTER, DEIRDRE,
with appreciation for her extraordinary support
and valuable criticism.

*   *   *

I wish to thank my much beloved friend, the late Joris Brinkerhoff,
for his help in editing the manuscript,
and my daughter, Laura
who encouraged my efforts
and Marni Sinclair for her photograph
of our *"going"*.

CONTENTS

While Walking On Sanibel Island..xi

LOVE IN THE TIME OF OLD AGE

A Note From Madrid.....................1
One Definition.............................2
Mapping A Terrain.......................2
Analyses.....................................3
On The Other Hand.....................3
A Matter Of Geography 4
Out Of Work...............................4
Don Juan At Shady Rest..............4
Unrequited Love.........................5
The Skylight 5
Recovery....................................6
How Like A Rose.........................6
Lunch 7
An Old Bird.................................7
Balance......................................8

About Gems................................8
Estrangement..............................9
Private Lives..............................10
Joint Custody............................10
Finality.....................................10
A Season's Close........................11
The Recurring Tense..................11
Once Upon A Time.....................13
The Morning After The Night
Before 14
Hibernation 14
Alas!...15
On Wings Of Song.....................15
Learning By Imitation................16

ON THE DARK SIDE

The View From My Belmont
Window 17
Classical Tragedy.......................18
Pages That Are Missing 18
My Mother's Farewell To St.
Joe..19
The Power Of Remnants 19
Making It Easy On The Family 20
Only If The First Death Is Your
Own..21

Résumé 21
After The Fact 22
Parting......................................22
Poor Butterfly............................23
After The End Of The Main
Event..23
Recalling 1969...........................24
Annuals In Flight.......................24
A Subliminal Call 25
Mind Over Faith........................25

Membership

Matriarchal Gallery 27

Conversations With My
Children...............................28

Alienation...............................28

Family Reunion 29

A Mother's Complaint.................30

Photographs.................................30

Without Choice............................31

The Silence Maker 31

To A Scholar Who Travels A
Lot..32

When To Reap?.............................32

Calling Gramma...........................33

My Glasses 34

Telephone Terrorist 34

In Search Of A Happy Ending...35

A Few Stops Along The Way

Around a Pool In Arizona...........37

With Dante At Squaw Peak........38

An Exhibition of Picasso's Stick
Line Drawings At the Phoenix
Museum..................................39

Accountability..............................39

Affluence Without Feathers...... 40

One More Last Stand................. 40

A Gardener..................................41

A Farewell Party...........................41

Returning To Home Base...........42

Transplant 42

Under A Full Moon......................43

New Hampsire Camp....................43

Kitty's Garden 44

Missing A Garden........................ 44

Mrs. Gardner's Garden............... 44

One Investment Strategy............45

Interiors 45

Music 46

Art In Trade 46

Making A Patio 47

A Return To My Cape House ... 48

Rememberlng A Cape Cod
Hurricane 49

Capers In Mid-Winter.................49

A Day At The Cape 50

New Hampshire From A Car
Window 51

A Condominium's Lake 51

Ducks And Women......................52

The Club.......................................52

A Florida Waiting Game.............52

Policy Is Everything.....................53

Florida Rv Park............................54

Hurricane Alley 55

About Poetry

Trying To Make It Clear.............57

Poetry In The Witness Chair.....57

Oh, To Be A Cormorant! 58

Across A Divide.............................58

A Box Of Tools 59

From A Kitchen Table 59

The Crux Of The Matter.............59

Out Of The Workshops Into The
Sun 60

To Be A Poet 61

Choices 61

The Cultivation Of My
Universe............................62

Attica................................62

Writing In Florida 63

Enough Already!................63

On And Off The Cape.............64

The Renaissance....................64

The Crab Knows........................64

Where Life Begins.....................66

The Nature Of Destiny.............67

On Behalf Of Poetry (I, II, III,
IV,) 68

A Simile...................................70

Chicago! Chicago!

From Tall Buildings To Small
Places...............................71

Christmas In Chicago 71

There, But For The Grace Of
Chance, Go I.........................72

Christmas Eve 73

Closing In On My Return
Ticket................................73

When Wings Finally Close

A Little Boy Will Ask.................75

In Retirement 75

Common In The Common........76

A Gardener Lays Down Her
Hoe 76

Withdrawal 77

Winter's Watch..........................77

Life According To Life 78

Shady Rest..............................78

A Right Denied 79

It's A Horse Race.........................79

The Theater...........................80

Not Everyone's Beach Day 80

The Loss Of An Old Friend 81

Friendship In Old Age.............82

What's Her Name........................82

One More Loss..........................83

That Time Of Year 83

Born Again 84

An Easy Way Out........................85

No Futures Contract 85

Historical Relevance...................86

Who Am I In All Of This?.........87

As A Moth Would Do 87

Just The Way Things Are 88

Ah! Were It But So.......................89

The Great Power..........................90

Facing Up 91

The Comfort Of Darkness.........92

On The Edge Of Each Cliff........93

Possibilities 95

To Die By Choice.........................95

Two Together Are Better Than
One 96

So—What Else Is New?.............96

Carnival Cruise...........................96

NPR..97

Retirement 98

While Walking On Sanibel Island

I *am an auditor,*
an ambivalent observer
of countless congregations
repeating their verses.
Numbed by doubt,
I turned to audit simpler things.
I watched two egrets
lace the air
into a curve of feathers.
Can the rush I heard replace
the Word, the syllables of faith?
As I watched two egrets bent upon
the multiplication of nests,
I did not question the curve of nature.

LOVE IN THE TIME OF OLD AGE

A Note From Madrid

Is it the wine that brings you here
far from the place I left behind?
Is it from wine that I digress
from all the beauty I have seen?
El Greco, Goya, Velázquez,
the calming Dutch with their families,
Picasso, Miró, Delacroix.
As I think of what I have seen,
I compare my love for beautiful things
to the rapture I felt at your touch.
Is it the art that invades my thighs
with urgent want transcending sight?
If it's not the art then it's you, my love,
who follows me both day & night.

One Definition

Love is an amorphous bridge,
probably ten feet wide,
eight feet high
and a thousand feet deep.
It's made of spirit,
connecting you to where he is,
him to where you are.
That the bridge is amorphous
presents no danger
since those in love
are weightless.

Mapping A Terrain

The ambivalence I feel
about love & loving comes and goes.
Retrospect—the teacher of doubt.
The present—an optimist.
The future—unreliable.

Analyses

Infatuation warmed the hours
between his coming and his going.
Desire like a golden arrow hit the mark.
Passion bloomed upon our flesh,
bred the longing sex inspires
when sex begins, bred wonder
at its happening!
But alas, we were too old
with memories that competed
with the infancy of *us.*
Too old to build experience,
to share the look of things
surrounding a lifetime of taste.
Too old to make a past to laugh about,
or to reveal what once was private.

On The Other Hand

She arrived at the border of life
where children became her circle.
Her husband left her passionless,
or so she says.
Thus, she has no need for love
beyond familial ties.
Old heart, do you not sense the siphon
draining life that does not use
what life has yet to offer?

A Matter Of Geography

Unlike the rush of midwest rivers
that eases the yearning plains,
his love was dry
unable to nurture what love requires
to grow beyond desire.

Out Of Work

Solitude becomes my age,
an age where jewels
no longer flatter.
Love has retired.
It works no more.
Time is empty
of all but space
that cannot echo
what did not last.

Don Juan At Shady Rest

His heart is sad as roses grieve
the loss of summer's flair.
His heart is numb with a plastic hose
that circulates a cautious stream.
Wondering where his lovers went,
leaving him in his old age,
he fondles the nerve-end of desire
while he waits for an aid to bring him his pills.

Unrequited Love

As with the flip side of a coin,
one of us was bound to lose.
That one was I.
Though unrequited love is stored
deep in the flesh of a lover's heart,
tremors of want yet palpitate
like a throbbing field in late October
when bloom is a thing barely recalled
even as trees weep for the past.

The Skylight

My room is open to the moon in its nightly course.
Last night, its fullness lit the end of love.
My sight restored, my mind recovering importances,
I lay beside him, aging with indifference.
The moonlight bathed his whiteness,
gave him the look of death.
My tan beside his pallor emphasized it.
I disengaged from his leg, grown possessive during the night,
then went to the bathroom to dress.
Impatient to start my day, I rattled pans
as I prepared love's farewell breakfast.

Recovery

Last summer at the Grand Canyon,
I did not imagine his face
enlivening a tomb of rock.
Nor did echoes recall his music,
nor the Canyon recall the Cape.
It was a beginning.
I left the Canyon for Phoenix.
Arriving there, I flushed desert sand
between my toes, felt sand as sand
not as an imperative metaphor.

How Like A Rose

Looking out at the garden,
I imagine myself as an ovary
in the luxury motel of a rose.
How close I could get
to a flower's scent
if I could invent a carrier
as bright as a bee
to transport seed
to the center of my habitat.

Lunch

Let's have lunch and speak of times
when hunger was still sharp
and passion undiminished.
Let's have lunch and peel those plumbs
of appetite that once inspired
delicious yearning.
But over coffee, will we pause
before the absence of desire?
And after lunch in our old age,
rather like leaves as they renounce
the rapture of summer,
mightn't we find "goodbye" is easy?

An Old Bird

Aging birds flutter and mutter
of kids & wills & inheritance.
Too cautious to keep to the pace of lust,
they slow their passage down.
An old bird flies too low for love,
fearful of heights.

Balance

I never knew a man
So well equipped
with the balance it takes
to sit on a fence.

About Gems

Love is a jewel one should not cut.
Faceted edges risk the core
when lovers insist on brilliance
in a stone worn out from wear.

Estrangement

"What shall we talk about
if not about the weather,
or how your office works,
or if grandchildren will graduate
with honors from the Ivy League
or fail to be what we expected
Do we count too much on it,
our bland participation?
Reviewing what we meant to be
to one another in the beginning,
do we fully understand
what happened between us?
Why shouldn't I ask the question
that has troubled me over the years?"
Her husband looked up from his book.
Defending the past, he cautioned her,
"We are too old to talk
of disappointment or of pain.
What could have been so terrible
when after all, back then, we let it pass.
We let it pass like the time of day."
But looking back, she asked herself:
Did love simply cease to speak,
or had it gone away?

Private Lives

A scarlet runner is a vine,
a rapid climber from a tender root
and difficult to transplant.
People, like plants, are limited
by what their growth requires.
Some, like the scarlet runner,
spend short-lived lives of bloom
climbing walls too high to carry
spliced appendages on their backs.

Joint Custody

Men & women can cultivate
gardens of unique designs,
agreeable to each.
But only if they give & take
for patterns they devise
in partnership.

Finality

I save love's remnant,
a tattered rag of what was once
the garment of my life.
But changing clothes is what we do.
I should take the rag and bury it.
Buy something new.

A Season's Close

As this season closes,
illuminating consciousness,
we'll have no reason to offend,
avoiding questions to the end.
Absent from each other's skin,
grown tender with each passing year,
love has become an abstraction,
white on white without a title.

The Recurring Tense

Here I go again, lamenting
The past, drawn to action
By memories of pain,
Pain that filters through loss,
Attributing to grammar
Inevitability:
That love is a verb, forever moving,
Forever moving away from itself.

An Ailing Giant

Strapped to disease,
he keeps to a chair
in front of TV.
Diabetes limits abilities.

His legs no longer carry his feet
with any degree of confidence.
His fingers can't pick up the pill
he accidentally drops.

He shuffles about his little room,
he, who'd performed throughout the world,
recalling a tune he once played.
The party's over, my friends.

Once Upon A Time

So long ago it was. For such a long time
you were the measure that scored desire
transposed into the poems I wrote.
Seeing you now, down for the count,
fragile in wit and slow to move,
I remember you back to what you were,
a king—swinging on a keyboard,
the center of a beat for such a long time.

After seeing you in Providence, I left for the South,
still lost in a dream remembering
you and the nights of listening,
driving down Route 28, high on anticipation,
a bottle of Gallo at my side just in case you'd say,
"Go get a life for Christ's sweet sake."
But where are you? What is the fate
you've encountered?
Where am I? Here on a beach with my pacemaker.

A Limitation

I've loved too much
that which manipulates reality.
I love the world, the friends I've had.
I love my children.

But I loved too much what can't be had
within the boundaries of ideal,
and loved too little what might have been
had I but loved one man enough.

The Morning After The Night Before

I've climbed mountains of lust.
Enjoyed the summit, I will admit.
But reviewing the valley that lay below,
I yearned for the lush embrace of verse,
the words that come with solitude
after a storm has passed.

Hibernation

My lust is dreaming like a bear
absorbing winter into sleep.
Should it wake in search of honey,
I'd give my sweet tooth serious thought.
Though lust is helpful in writing verse,
it also takes a woman's time
and turns it into a servant.

Alas!

Far from dying of love, I have learned
one cannot warm one's backside
in a bed of cold ashes.

On Wings Of Song

I listened to a nightingale's
arioso in the meadow,
gracing the air with confidence
knowing the charm of its voice.

And I asked:

"Where do you fly sweet bird of song?
Where is your nest, the home of your longing?"
"Here in the meadow," the bird replied.
"Here where my true love flew and died."

Learning By Imitation

Because I do not wish to yearn again
Because I do not wish
Because I know I do not wish to yearn
As they, I will resist the time and place
Where love awaits to enter me.
Why should I mourn the closing of a door?
Why should I yearn for echoes of a door
Closing on pain?

    I am saddened
By the brave exploits of love
I do not care to be so brave again
To follow love into its last retreat
To linger there where memory holds
What wants free from love's power.
Because I know that bloom is seasonal
I can forgive its passing
For in every time and every place in time
Its root remains immutable.

    Because I know that pain is terminal
I will survive pain
And eat the last of what remains of it
As animals devour the sac that holds life.
Because I have loved, I love even more
The memory of past encounters
Stripped of all their blame, unable to commit
The last outrageous act of love
To leave into the terminal
Compound of grief.

Pray for us who love too much the messengers of pain.
Pray for us who grieve too much the passing of flowers.

ON THE DARK SIDE

The View From My Belmont Window

Branches are bare and thinly drawn
against the sky.
Arms sheathed in ice
clasp the air in a vice of cold.
Yet one can sense in torpid wood
a frozen stream in the trunk of trees
yearning toward liquidity.

How like the wood old age becomes
stripped of passion, its flame expired,
clinging to life with brittle arms.
In slowing night, stars disappear
as day resumes its bright opinion
consoling old age with light to come.

Distancing

I will never again believe
that conversation can mitigate
a careless word, once spoken.
Nor flatter myself again that I
can persuade events not to happen.
I'll never again contest with fate
for the misery that flows between
what is expressed & what is not
in a troubled sea of consciousness.

Classical Tragedy

When Achilles howled
at Patroclus' death,
he was called a sensitive hero.
When a woman howls for a cheated life,
she is called bitter.

Pages That Are Missing

Struggling within myself, I lost an opportunity
to understand my mother's times,
to listen to experience distinct from my own.

Her stories gone to earth,
I'm left with supposition where I might have heard
the history she'd have taught me had I but listened.

And history, parent to my past, is what is missing.
The loss of definition is what is missing.
Not of her alone, but of me.

My Mother's Farewell To St. Joe

A week before my mother died,
I drove her through the neighborhoods,
past her church, down to the beach
below her house, out to the countryside.

The orchards gnarled the winter sky.
Michigan's lake was gathering ice.
From her Congregational Church's spire,
a prescient bell tolled the hour.

The drive comprised a summary
of her life in that small town.
Seeing it lie in winter's quiet,
she closed her eyes & said goodbye.

The Power Of Remnants

It was in 1995 you made your impressive exit.
Green plastic bags were packed with your dresses,
your Davidow suits, your satin slips—et cetera,
and left at the door of the
Salvation Army's collection post.
But not your blouses, your Pendleton jacket, your scarves.
What is it in the touch of cloth
that holds me back from setting aside
what can't be altered by regret?

Making It Easy On The Family

I do not know what became
of the bronze urn my mother bought
for her ashes. No one followed it
to the family plot.

Cremation customizes death
to a package less onerous
than ritual requires.

We joined the congregation for lunch.
Then met with family at Mother's house
not yet aware of what we'd lost.

Only If The First Death Is Your Own

"After the first death there is no other."
One might as well say,
after the first dawn there is no other
or after first love there is no other.

The setting sun is indifferent
to the dark it makes with the loss
of each day's light.
Rising, it will set again. Death is like that.

Résumé

His body was dying behind his face,
behind the bravura of his talk.
For a year or so we saw no difference.
Then, morbidity began to show.
Death warns of its arrival,
warnings he didn't share with anyone
until it was too late.

After The Fact

One learns to accept the cycle
indicated at birth,
that the gift of life is terminal,
as terminal as these may be:
The poetry in art,
innovation through ideas,
the swirl of language & of paint,
the love of God through nature.
All of these may pass. And yet,
I hope for permanence.
It is the irony of disbelief.

Parting

Parting goes so far away
spreading out from yesterday
down beyond the last tomorrow
echoing, "I can't forget."

Poor Butterfly

Dead butterflies like memories
huddle beneath dead leaves,
they who passed sweet messages
from flower to flower.

Pity the butterfly whose wings you tear
and thorax you split when you mount its carcass
on a piece of cardboard under glass.
Pity the butterfly caught in flight.

After The End Of The Main Event

I would speak to you as I did once
when the scent of lilacs filled the air
with spring's denial of winter's proof.
I would share with you a moment
as it moves across the garden disturbing roots.

I would not ask you stay beyond
the advent of memory. I would not ask
for the warmth of touch nor the look of you.
I would only ask that you enter my mind
and speak to me as you did once.

Recalling 1969

A tempest came to Cambridge
then limped away as children do
muttering a cheap contempt.
And like the parents of our past
we fitted glass back to the sills,
swept the ways & paid the bills.

Annuals In Flight

April's liquor wakes roots for spring's revival,
intoxicates the earth.
Rain stirs the seed beds of my garden,
wakes memories of annuals that won't return.

In April, I dream of my brother, of
his dangerous courage in ignoring
a controller's warning as he flew his
family south.
His Comanche's wings, clipped by
ice, couldn't lift the plane above Rip
Mountain in Tennessee.
When the mountain released its giant snow,
it melted their bodies as well.

How often we meet & speak of them.
But the tears we shed that April
no longer flood remembrance.
Time & earth absorb their losses,
bookkeepers without sentiment.

A Subliminal Call

No threat of Death's coming dampens
my wonder, though I grew cautious
and moved to the South.
Steeling my soul against his call,
I keep to the sun, talk to a child,
Watch a southern garden grow.

Mind Over Faith

Myth is made by the awesome need
of all mankind to bow before
omnipotence. A power that gives
through absolute faith
what mankind cannot promise.

We have the earth. Should it not be
a changing picture of what we are
in a universe whose mysteries
compel man's intellect to search?
But then we ask, what tames the beast?

MEMBERSHIP

Matriarchal Gallery

Was the matriarch benign
who hung their pictures in a line,
the children of her family?

She framed them early in their lives,
containing them in rigid squares
so they would hang correctly.

Conversations With My Children

How sweet the sound of love,
sweetness condensing language
as dew on an iron fence
drips jewels on the coming grass.

Our copper lined conversations
shorten the distance I require
to scribble verses few will read.
But scribbling is what I do.

One day, I'll leave this lonely place
to join you in your separate lives.
Will conversation then be less
than what it was on telephones?

And will the sound of love remain
as I grow weak, have need of help?
Or will the dew from an iron fence
no longer flatter the coming grass?

Alienation

His hand limps toward
anemic couplings.
His gaze is what *The Wasteland*
teaches, dimly understood.
I cannot fathom
the flint-point of his anger.
Thus it is, without intention,
I offend.

Family Reunion
for Marsha D.

The family meets once a year
for close encounters on fifty-three acres
in the middle of Vermont.
Each with a point of view:
Husband on wife, wife on kids,
adults on the in-laws,
grandchildren pushing speech.

Language invades alliances,
disturbing the equilibrium
of accustomed space & practices
in contrast to an orchestra
that allows each section its voice.

Who edits the score for the liberated child
whose instrument still screeches?
Who writes the lyrics for an aging parent
who would like some help in the kitchen,
or for the conductor who can't direct
the intricacies of counterpoint
but won't give up the baton?

Illusion is the mending tape
each uses on returning home
exhausted by the bond of blood.
Still—the following year they will return
each needing to play in an orchestra
whose dissonance may never resolve,
but which plays the only tune they know.

A Mother's Complaint

A caretaker touches too much dirt
to gain respect from the dirt makers.

A mother's mask is pasted together
in conversations away from her table.

The mask is affixed to a face they recall
but not so clearly as the mask they've made.

Photographs

I face photographs I have hung
on the wall beyond my desk:
The celluloid sum of who I am
in photos of my parents,
my sister & my brother,
my daughters & my son.

They are as giant wombs easing out
the inventories of their minds.

Pain, intrinsic to the task
is scratched upon their faces
in lines of disappointment,
pride, in lines of work that
do not fade
with anyone's accomplishment,
in lines of simply growing old.

Without Choice

Confronted with Hobson's choice,
she studied at the Cordon Bleu
to understand how a mousse can run.

She gave up art as survivors do
when life is short of cash. She knew
that poverty's no fun. Forgetting art,

she settled for two-week vacations
away from the kitchen that fed her purse,
gave her a pension & health insurance.

The Silence Maker

Come a little closer
and I will take your pulse
to determine
if you are still alive in spite of it.

It has been the problem
seething between us.
It the monster silence
digesting our meanings.

To A Scholar Who Travels A Lot

Being a scholar who travels a lot,
you'll witness the evil man perpetrates
against the world he plunders.
Thus greed challenges virtue
while love is a modest hope
against the reign of Diabolus,
who also travels a lot.

When To Reap?

One day, perhaps he'll no longer wish
to be laid back upon the past
like a dead bouquet,
but spread his bloom about the world
casting seed in the usual way.

Calling Gramma

Hi, Gramma. It's me, Joanne.
What do you mean?
Don't you remember
what I said?

I'm sending back the money.
I'll never end my debt to you
but this one I can pay.

No. Jimmy's in a private school.
They keep him there til six o'clock.
That's when I'm able to pick him up.

My place? But I've got to work.
It's nice there, Gramma. He's O.K.

I'm sorry you're not well.
I'll call you later.

I'm fine. Don't worry. Him?

No, not any more.
I don't want to talk about it.
Try to understand.

Oh, Gramma, don't start.
I'll call you soon.
I've got to run. Yes, I'll call Mom,
later—when I can.

My Glasses

I wear glasses.
I am mother. I've been daughter.
I've looked far. I look near.
But in between
I wonder what I've missed.

Telephone Terrorist

The telephone rings.
"You know who I am.
I want to sit on your face."
She calls the police.
They make a report.
The telephone rings.
The line is open but no one speaks.
She checks the doors,
inspects the windows.
The locks are old.
She calls her mother,
asks her if she wants to visit.
The telephone rings.
She does not answer.
Tomorrow, she'll have
her number changed.

In Search Of A Happy Ending

Returning home from a business trip,
she met a man with extremely blond hair.
By the time they arrived in Boston,
they'd established a mutual attraction
and arranged dates on their calendars
to further the relationship.

One Sunday he proposed they go to the Cape
so she could meet his parents
who played golf at a club called *Wianno*.
She stroked his very blond hair streaked
with implications of private beaches
& restricted clubs, then jumped out of bed,
rushed to her phone & bought a ticket to Amsterdam.

Perhaps, in the air she would meet what lies
between the wasp-infested suburbs & the political left.
The tip-off to a modest, intelligent,
self-supporting male was what?
An open laptop? A briefcase full of papers?
The New Yorker & *The Paris Review* resting on his lap,
The Nation & *The Economist* balancing the act?
Or would it be an uncommitted stare out of the window?

While Walking The Apache Trail

So often left behind,
An old friend is like a seed
Cast upon the wind in a previous spring
That waited in affection's soil
To express its fertility.

A FEW STOPS ALONG THE WAY

Around a Pool In Arizona

I saw what I thought was a sad old man,
a lonely and distracted man
taking the sun around the pool
never speaking to anyone.
One day I approached him.
I found he was not shy at all.
He spoke of early planting
in Manitoba where he farmed.

He rose and pointed out his wife,
knitting a sweater by the pool.
He was taller than I by a foot or so
and smiled easily.
"We have a lot of fun," he said.
"Our children will be coming soon."
I'm glad he wasn't a sad old man.
I liked the way he stood.

With Dante At Squaw Peak

Resting at the quarter mark,
I met a man with a very sore foot
massaging his sole. We started to chat.
Perhaps it was that, his very sore foot,
that led him to speak of the war,
of how long he had marched to do what he did.
His story was an aftershock
of what I'd heard before.

When he'd finished, we looked down on Phoenix.
A shimmering abstraction in summer's heat,
it lay like a snake coiling in the sun
preparing to strike. I continued to climb
to the top of Squaw Peak. When I looked below,
I saw the man wearing his shoes in a painful descent.

An Exhibition of Picasso's Stick Line Drawings At the Phoenix Museum

Some men say:
"Women are unable to digest the fruits
of our philosophies.
Unable to discern the tragedy of spring,
of birds returning to shattered nests,
of the fall whose blood lingers in the cups of leaves,
of ideas that anchor conversation
(unlike the prattle of our wives),
or of winter that impounds our everlasting souls."

Some women say:
"We are the makers of men's comfort,
the conservators of their pride,
their caretakers from the bridal path to the grave.
We engage their passion.
We are part of a slave trade romanticized by custom.
Yet some men, like Picasso, throw darts at a gate
they either envy or despise."

Accountability

Most men need to fence their labor.
Not always out of vanity
but as graphics in a summary.
It's the catalog of ownership,
their itemized accomplishments
that give most men their certainty.

Affluence Without Feathers

In spring summer and fall,
thousands flock to Santa Fe
to peer upon the Pueblo face.
To shop for pots & rugs & silver
from an Indian culture gone public.

Soon a casino will take the place
of artisans with burnt-out eyes.
But China will resuscitate
a dying romance, trading for dollars
with cheap imitations of America's past.

One More Last Stand

Hopis return to sacred soil
at the end of life.
They arrive there promptly
so as not to miss
the only path that Hopis take
leaving the songs of earth.

And every tree will bow its branches,
every flower nod in sadness,
and all the wolves & mighty bears,
the flocks of sheep & flocks of birds,
all creatures of Hopi land will watch
as a Hopi returns to earth.

A Gardener

I putter in the country
in the company of birds.
I'm a very boring person,
in case you haven't heard.

A Farewell Party

Two pearls float upon my lobes
reminding me
of the kindness I received
with pearls & wine
on a Sunday afternoon.
We were there to say goodbye.
We drank too much as people do
softening experience.

Too talkative for conversation,
we slurred upon the surfaces.
Finally, we said goodbye.
No one wishing to sustain
an altered situation.
No one wishing to remain
beyond an empty glass.

Returning To Home Base

I have returned after many years
to the town of my life with family.
Driving about, I see the houses
that belonged to my friends,
friends who have died or moved away.

How placid they sit, the houses I've known,
undisturbed by change.
Houses are not sentimental.
They belch up families into vans
without shedding a drop of paint.

Transplant

Stacked upon shelves of polished glass,
geraniums bloom almost as well
as they did last summer,
planted in my garden's warm, manured earth.

Occasionally, an overcast sky
obscures the light they feed upon.
At which time, I turn on a switch
and food pours down from the ceiling.

Under A Full Moon

The barbecue pit is covered with leaves
frozen into molds of mulch.
Ice on walks intimidates
the range of aging hips.

Walking in a windless night,
one can hear snow crunch underfoot,
its echo rising to an innocent moon
that views the world below as safe.

New Hampsire Camp

The mice are unafraid.
Chipmunks prowl on window sills.
Cracked nuts divide my lingerie.
Droppings fill my shoes.

Summer comes after spring
(at least, I think it does),
unless the spring just lingers on
till the Fourth of July,
when winter begins.

Kitty's Garden
for Kitty W.

Late in the day she wanders down
from garden chairs into the sweet
cut grass and deep into the flocks
of bloom, perennials, annuals,
and one pink bed of roses.
An artist in the ways of earth,
she plants her pictures, as did Monet.

Missing A Garden

My neighbors pass by, I assume
looking for gardens finer than mine,
since as they go, they do not pause
to remark on the weather or to say,
"How fine your roses are this year."
Earphones in place, too busy to stop,
they miss the conversation that
a garden makes. Nor do they see
the symptoms of summer crowding beds,
nor do they hear God's whisper.

Mrs. Gardner's Garden

Isabella planted them on the walls
of her villa in a clutter of ownership
without concern for height or light.

And not too far from the Boston Museum
whose gardener left space between the rows.
Where light could enter and warm the paint.

One Investment Strategy

A phoebe nested behind the shade
of my porch light. While she was scratching
for a worm, I demolished her house.
But she returned with firm resolve.

The phoebe is small but diligent.
And though her nest had been destroyed,
she thought her next design would be
safe from wind & misguided bats.

How simple the phoebe's plan for life
as year after year with her birdie brain
she zeros in on that same porch light
to build, rebuild, rebuild again

Interiors

I look about me.
Thrift store art covers my walls,
exudes the warmth I need for comfort.
It's pretty cheap to fill one's space
with someone else's cast off art
if you shop at the Salvation Army,
consignment stores with 'sale' signs,
or even at your local dump.
It's pretty cheap & cheap is prudent
when one considers the history of tulips.

Music

Taken from an inner voice,
Music repeats
On the dome of a singer's throat,
In columns of air from reeds and strings.
Each borrowing from genius
Embedded lines of sound
To express what words cannot.

Art In Trade

No art teaches the life of a city
As does the Greek urn.
They were not the creation of aristocratic taste,
But the skill of craftsmen observing their world.
Vases thrown by the masters of mud
Were exported like gold by Athenians in trade
As art & commerce intertwined
To tell the story of Attica.

Making A Patio

The brick is falling into place
row after row. Soon I will sit
on a patio designed by
a mason who knows his craft.
My neighbors quit their walks to watch
a skilled mason laying brick.
Diligence in learning how
a thing is put together,
turns a man into a master.
Turns his work into art.

A Return To My Cape House

Missing the Cape, I returned
to my Centerville house
where I was forced to face the blight
from protracted deferments.
I called in a carpenter.

He gave me a rough estimate
of what he would charge
to replace the windows,
shore up the porch,
turn over-ripe shingles,
install a new roof.
God only knows what the paint job will cost.

Returning to the Cape
has burdened my budget.
When the work is finished,
I'm going to tack a "For Sale" sign up
on a very expensive plastic fence.

Remembering A Cape Cod Hurricane

Hip roses hugged the fragile shore,
bound the wounds from sand & water.
Front yards that had boasted
countless shade
then had to face the uprooted.
Throughout the Cape the "cats" were out
pulling stumps & clearing rubble.
But in spite of the havoc the storm inflicted,
along the path to Craigville beach
buttercups flourished in charming reminders
that summer forgives.

Capers In Mid-Winter

The wind steals beneath the siding,
whines and enters through the wrap,
makes the aging windows tremble
as wind finds space along the sashes.
Capers curl into their houses,
hoping fires up narrow chimneys
can dissipate what winter brings
after a ten week season.

A Day At The Cape

I had just come from Boston and though it was late,
I decided to walk to Craigville Beach.
I'd know I was back on the Cape
when I touched the lace of Nantucket Sound.

Waltzing in the low tide foam, seaweed slunk,
its hair unfurled to slimy roots
sucking the marrow of rocks.

Wandering along the lisping shore
scuffing shells, collecting a few,
I felt the softness of Cape air
as it wound its spell around me.

When the tide began to turn,
I knew it was time to leave the beach.
But before I left, I buried a six-pack
in the sand like a bone I could later retrieve.

The Cape is warm at sunset
with its captives huddled in bars,
on decks or patios,
lifting glasses to the very rascal
that's charmed them from reality.

It's an Irish trick.

It's hard to leave the beach,
harder still to leave the Cape.
Crossing the bridge at Sagamore,
I pulled very hard against gravity.

New Hampshire From A Car Window

I am too old to hold the present.
It balloons into confusion.
But my yesterdays had moments
that mitigate their passing.

Driving through Hancock, I recalled the past
which seemed more present than the current day.
Summer lazing on the little town's lake.
Autumn waiting for the call of the loon.

The sweet congruence of talk and friendship
with Elinor & Madolyn.
The changing light on Norway Hill.
Town meetings. Small happenings.

I admired the modesty
of a town whose borders had not strayed
into the surrounding woodland,
but had tied its apron close around.

A Condominium's Lake

I look out on a man-made lake,
a developer's attempt
to imitate nature with surface water
Still, it's water,
and water is something
worth looking at.

Ducks And Women

A Muscovy chick stirs the pond,
rippling the lake's glassy surface.
Water quivers like satin cut
on the bias a woman wears
who understands its purpose.
Everything follows from small events.
The chick has left its mother
to test a depth where turtles live.
A woman leaves her mother
to cut a bolt of cloth.

The Club

We're members of a club,
"The Old Ladies Club".
And Maria is our champion,
The beautiful Haitian greeter
At the Walmart where we shop.

A Florida Waiting Game

Like a snake avoiding the heat
when summer comes,
he keeps to the shade
of his air-conditioned room,
watches TV, waits for fall
when a snow bird might perch
on his palsied palm
and relate to his
Sunbeam hand vibrator.

Policy Is Everything

The garden is new, bought at Home Depot
just days ago—nothing from seed
to delay the view from my patio.

My Florida garden makes no promise
it can't keep, unlike New England's waking beds,
decisions of spring parsing plots, seedlings
hardened to survive an untimely frost.

Life born in darkness, nurtured by care
quartered by the seasons of its passion,
gives calendars significance, as northern gardens
make dates with cycles in adventures with hope.

Here in Florida, plants may die
If I drop them on their heads, tear their roots,
or if my dog digs them out of bed,
or if immortal bugs eat them alive.

But then, I'll return their remains to Home Depot
and get my money back.

Florida Rv Park

What draws me from
the frantic sociability of the trailer park?
In Florida, I read in *The Boston Globe*
that their winter is long & hard this year.

Then why can't I dance in peace
having learned the steps,
having earned my keep?

Why should I leave the Ping-Pong match
to exercise in solitude?
What more is there to hollow
from the igloo of my loneliness?

Well, the dance is repetitious
and Ping-Pong has its limits.
But watching fireflies spark the boonies,
perhaps, I'll write a poem tonight.

Hurricane Alley

The hurricane season is upon us.
It takes six months to resolve the urge
of mighty winds as they swell & grow
on the Gulfs warm water.
It takes six months for nature to tire
of the dark side of wind at work.

Tornadoes will rip the seashore apart.
Fragile metal residences
that fill trailer parks will be yanked from their ties,
lifted & dumped like so much trash.
Home owners prepare
with plywood on windows or hurricane shutters
to protect them against attacks on glass.

Snakes & 'gators & water rats
will clutter the flood, invading streets.
Gambler's losses must then be cleaned up
as insurance companies question claims
while the governor claims disaster.
Those who remain in Florida shoot craps
with the Caribbean, betting their houses
in rolls against the vagaries of weather.

ABOUT POETRY

Trying To Make It Clear

It's an attempt at lucidity,
insisting the thing said
be as clearly stated
as understanding through language
can manage to do.
This practice, most appropriate to prose,
makes commonplace,
a song sung by a nightingale.

Poetry In The Witness Chair

Poetry is witness
to complaisance in the spirit
which slouches in a grownup's chair
and lets the toys of youth drift by
losing the clarity of things once seen
by a child before it ages.

Oh, To Be A Cormorant!

A cormorant can fly, float in branches,
bewitch the world with an evil eye
without regard for its reputation.
But I'm no bird, no cormorant,
to spread my wings like a canopy
over a nest of seaweed—self assured.

I'm a poet, a woman alone,
who spends old age scribbling verse,
critically aware that a poem must fly.
I should have been a cormorant
able to soar with a catch in my beak
after plumbing deep water for shadows.

Across A Divide

She was eighteen when I met her.
Experience divided us.
Yet, the arts we each explore
arrived between her age & mine
as if we both were children
meeting at a playground.

A Box Of Tools

A box of newly sharpened pencils
is open on my desk.
I use them tip by tip as though
their points had special powers.

The smell of lead is on my fingers
which indicates that I'm at work
taking a poem from atmosphere
with pencils that mark the dew point.

From A Kitchen Table

Each poem is a loaf she shapes
then bakes. A part of herself
glazes the surface making crust
to protect the dough from itself.
After the loaf is baked and cooled,
she shares it with her daughter
whose appetite bridges the chasm
of a generational gap.

The Crux Of The Matter

Creativity gives proof
that sex is worth the having,
its energy the vital source
of all that wants expression.

Out Of The Workshops Into The Sun

Their poems are like the brush of a leaf against air,
touch without proof flowing through the vein
of creativity.
Each poem is a secret they cup in their minds
then release like a fledgling pushed from its nest.
Thousands & thousands of poems they've written
urged by the passion that drives them,

unable to stop except to listen, to touch, to search
for what lies beyond perception. As
they migrate through the wilderness
from Cambridge to the Coast,
through the pain of writing without success
in the eyes of other poets,

still they endure to wash their feet
in a sea-bound stream and follow a turn
that ends the winding.
As they wander out of Kansas
through Iowa to Oregon,
they record the earth—its inhabitants,

not as carpet sweepers
whisking experience to unnatural clean,
but as builders framing for images.

The poets may write of the spider's lunch,
or of the miasma that emanates
from the corpse of chance.
But, they also write of Love (cynically or not),
and the importance of a snail's
progress through the grass.

To Be A Poet

There are a few who pass the test
that markets require of gift. Most do not.
A few climb the steps of a pyramid
and, like Cortez rocked by surmise,
realize America. They are the citizen-poets,
the masters of belonging,
the Whitmans of tomorrow.

Choices

Work is jealous as it competes
with social events surrounding friendships.
Language grows shy in my old age.
To scratch a few lines on the wall of my cave
ain't easy.

And then occurs the sameness of things—
the lunches, the dinners, the numbing drinks,
friends uttering the same information becoming
lost lines of verse to a social event.

The Cultivation Of My Universe

The continent of my being lies deep within the earth.
I moved to the country to imagine it more clearly.

Tides of wild grass washed the fields beneath my feet.
The songs of birds, a cantata to the shriek from city streets.

And I thought:
How beautiful the country, my
universe secure,
with all the baggage of my past in a
mound of rich manure.

And I wrote and I wrote and I wrote till
the pile decomposed,
then laid me down upon the grass
and watched the flowers grow.

Attica
For Ruth K

Memory floats throughout my books
of photographs from the trips we took.
The time we walked up a Grecian hill
to the Parthenon and Athena's niche
where elegant pillars yet survive
the weight of time & acid rain.

How bravely they stand,
those battered giants from a golden age
that once enlightened centuries
of art & politics & poetry,
for the *glory that was Greece!*

Writing In Florida

Here I am in shorts and halter
tanning as I type before a bank of
bougainvillea, the sun full on my back.
But warming under Apollo's sign
won't thaw the ice that coats my verse.
Snow birds follow the sun.
Winter has followed me.

Enough Already!

It is as though my incidents were important
to a reader miles away
from the tiny spaces inhabited by
moments from my past.
But what else should I write about?
What subject is more pertinent
than I am to myself?
Why expose my ego
to a failed transcendence
when I have words enough
to eulogize my past?

On And Off The Cape

Anticipation eased the strife
of driving down Route 3,
down to the shore of Nantucket Sound
where I'd be delivered of a child
out of an old necessity.

I was there once more and would remain
until the child grew tired of words,
the metered yearning the sea inspires,
an old love revising verse.
I was there to stay till the child died.

The Renaissance

It matters not what wilderness
they came from.
It's the planting that counts,
the cultivation accomplished
after centuries of drought.

The Crab Knows

Walking along Fort Myer's beach,
I watched sandcrabs scurry
then burrow into hermitage
to keep them safe for one more day.
And I wondered:
Am I no more than these
who do not question but retire
without a question into sand?

Slender Volumes

In the final analyses,
nothing changes between birth & death,
nothing that alters the design of a book.
All that a poet seeks to say,
gathered and sewn to a stable spine
for a slender volume with an elegant cover,
is no more valued than a cheap paperback,
no more enduring than a reader's interest.

What clue to immortality
resides in publication? What quality of print
is required for a text to survive?
What finer volume must then follow?
Something other than our limitations
surely bears the blame as we ask our muse,
our confident:
"Hey, you! You up there in Helicon!
Why do you clutter the freeway with signs
I cannot read and that lead to nowhere?"

Where Life Begins

In the spring when buds balloon sensing light
and monarchs hang enclosed in royal green,
the passion of earth breeds constituents for life.
Branches bend heavy, labor starts as trees renew
vague promises to spring,
and the white scream of winter is forgot.
A neighborly sun warms the gullible earth
and we, the sunshine poets, scribble lines
that dribble syrup on the truth.

How optimistic, poets denying
a corsage of grief. How sentimental
when the bleeding hearts of summer reveal
the melancholy in seasonal gifts!
To say how beautiful the garden now
that roses are in bloom and August looms
to perfume the night, decorate the parlor,
is callous in the face of those betrayed
by a garden's diminishment.

The Nature Of Destiny

Observing the river in Iowa City,
I sensed the flow of destiny,
not seeded as Iowa's soil is
but seeding on to another state
continuing the continent.

I knew the seed I had taken
from Iowa that other time
would grow as well in Florida,
New Hampshire or the Cape,
though not so well in cities.

On Behalf Of Poetry

I.

The tattered cloak of earth informs
the poet of his tragedy,
much as the flame of autumn consumes a feast.
And yet, and yet, a poet grieves
the absence of change, preferring death
to a Florida summer that never ends.

And yet, and yet, a poet regrets old age
as melancholy, the lens of fall,
limits size to a periscopic view.
Order, the center of a poet's vision,
then authors the significance of *me*.
The *me-ness* in the *is-ness* of things
then becomes the *is-ness* of what is.

II.

Poetry is inclined to please the ear
as music does without a word
(though making words from thinnest air).
Poetry speaks but not to reason,
to the undefined in the definite.
The sea, the sky, the alternating green,
red stains on the carpet
is what the poet sees & associates with *me*.

III.

How lacking in probity, the loss
of a village to corrupted fate.
How can poetry excuse
an unnatural declension
of life to death

or compensate for the loss of bloom
in the sunlit fields of youth?
Or is war a kind of resolution,
progress of a sort,
as nations redefine themselves,
indifferent to the cost.

Consider the Rubicon where Caesar crossed
to plunge his sword into the heart of Rome.
How many poets drink from that dark stream,
Vomit back mauve particles
of lost humanity.
What poet could resist the ardor of death,
the sex in brutality, the glory men esteem,
the holiness of sacrifice, the undying gleam
in a soldier's fixed eyes widened to express
a standard of honor and obedience?

IV.

In searching for the *is-ness* of things,
the essence of reality,
does poetry succeed where science fails
to dig below the surface?
We hand life over, each of us, to expertise
we cannot quiz. Question to the end game
as to what our moves should have been.
Confused and tired, we turn to poetry
(innocuous as poetry may be).
But if poetry were lost from the toolbox of language,
could science plane the ragged edge of grief?
or rebuild on the footings of tragedy?

A Simile

It was like summer on the Cape
or like frost on a window pane
where I had scratched a name
in water frozen on glass.

It was like October everywhere,
the perfect month with perfect days
holding the sweetness of the past
like Laura's eaten cherry pie.

It was like Chicago, burning
with activity & art.
Its passion built onto the sky
nicer than in Boston or New York.

It was like moments I have lived
with danger or tears or love.
It was like many things.
But as for it, itself, I haven't a clue.
It was like that.

CHICAGO! CHICAGO!

From Tall Buildings To Small Places

You can stand alone in Grant Park
or on a Michigan Avenue bridge
overlooking Chicago,
observing the elegance of design
and be grateful for the arts of nature & mankind.

Or, you may think that what you see
is the expression in God's eye
becoming one with mind & matter.
But, just how far would an eye cast its beam
even to design Michigan Avenue?

Christmas In Chicago

Chicago is terribly cold in the winter
testing courage as wind whips trees
and snow turns gray on city streets
for every sweet moment of white.
In the grip of the winter solstice,
a cautious sun stashes its gold
in a bank of encompassing ice.
And cancellations for flights heading south
are surely to be expected.
Chicago is terribly cold in the winter
but never boring & warm at night.

There, But For The Grace Of Chance, Go I

While in Chicago and having some time
before festivities got under way,
we went to the Art Institute,
revisited impressionists.
then followed the stairs down & around
to the American collection
filling the hour or so one spends
on a tour of familiar pictures.

Finally, I visited the lady's room.
I was washing my hands when I noticed
an attendant on my left, her eyes averted,
not meeting my gaze, a strained look of pride
confronting a woman-to-woman embarrassment.
As I put on my coat, she approached
to clean the wash bowl after me.

Walking up Michigan Avenue
admiring a jewel reset for Christmas,
I recalled the woman.
She'd placed no dish above the sink
in which a lady might leave some change.

Christmas Eve

The trim has been completed.
Perched upon the treetop,
a patriarchal Santa indicates the season.
Globes of gilded ornaments
against a kaleidoscopic string of lights
reflect the brightness of childhood
in dots & dashes squeezed between
a stratification of darkness.

Handel's *Alleluia* accompanies our joy
as we put away the clutter and clear
away the glasses for the next
day's celebration & the bonus we'll receive
for all the goodness we've performed
throughout this hectic, closing year.
For all the goodness we've performed,
we'll celebrate ourselves.

Closing In On My Return Ticket

Chicago is two days away
from being an unreality.
I'll soon be shopping at Walmart or Publix
(my Florida social experience),
and cleaning my condo for exercise.

Soon I'll be away, away from talk
with my very bright children,
away from their love, away from art,
away from the fall and from the spring,
away from it all, back into silence.

WHEN WINGS FINALLY CLOSE

A Little Boy Will Ask

The little boy asked,
"Are you afraid of dying?"
He'd seen an old man weep
and thought he wept for fear of death.
"Why no." I said. "The man you saw
may have suffered pain from a worn out back,
or maybe his dog had just been killed
by a passing truck. Something like that."
The boy thinks that life's a feast without flies.
He has not heard them buzzing yet
nor felt them on his eyes.

In Retirement

With the ozone layer ripped,
we keep to the shade, white as slugs,
avoid vacations at the beach.

For future health, we gave up junk
that clutters blood, smoke that kills,
booze & drugs that shorten life.

Afraid of AIDS, we gave up sex.
Afraid of the city we watch TV.
Afraid of planes we do not fly.

Common In The Common

Late in the afternoon they come,
read *The Globe,* play chess with regulars,
watch the sun make prisms on a field of glass.
Once isomorphic with the field,
now slivers on a city bench,
a generation yields.

A Gardener Lays Down Her Hoe

Her life, no more competing for a prize,
preferring now a quiet place
in which to meet a reckoning.
Her life, no more of interest, not to her,
condenses to a sigh.

She drags a chair across the lawn
to the cutting bed where zinnias brown.
As autumn begins its annual tour
she knows it's getting late.
The sun no longer warms her back.

The Time Keeper

I hear the clock more clearly now
where once it ticked *pianissimo*.
The pendulum is deeply etched,
valued more with each passing year.
In a major mode it notates a score
For an orchestra that plays a certain march.
Tick-tock, tick-tock, tick-tock.
And off I'll go.

Withdrawal

He has entered a wilderness
of mind without identity,
where once he had a name.
Though he is mute,
she strains to touch his silence,
to sign into feeling
where words no longer reach.

Winter's Watch

Paired in a fond boredom, they sit and wait.
No spring will swell, no season fill
the gap that saps their dreaming.
But their stories are old
and winter's rapping has a meaning.
She opens the draft, stirs the coals.
There is cake under glass.
For whatever passes, coffee is boiling.

Life According To Life

What does one want at the end?
Fine weather
the gathering of friends
not overlong
obeisance from the family
token gifts
hours of peace before TV
someone near
to watch the fading
occasionally to hear
the voices of the young
not fearing death
but wishing for an easy one
a cup of tea, small talk
a shawl against the draft
the comfort of familiar rooms
old photographs.
These one may have
with a modicum of life
if bread returns upon the water.

Shady Rest

Quaking at the edge of life,
she contemplates the end of it
as a traveler, weary of the sights
yearns to lay her baggage down.
But for questions without answers
she is cautious of change
like ripened fruit that does not fall
though it rots upon the vine.

A Right Denied

It was not their intent to wrestle with death,
to deny her escape from a body in pain,
but to keep her alive for a future event:
A wedding, a birth, a new addition
to the family house.
So they fed her and dressed her
and medicated sores, and tied
her to tubes and tied her to her bed.
All for her sake.

It's A Horse Race

Reminiscence scores the years.
No more to hear a lover's sigh.
No more to bear a market's trend.
No more regrets or hope for change.

Pills assist, my tests assure,
to keep life's urgent pace in check.
Acceptance, alone, can reign in despair
as one gallops toward the finishing post.

The Theater

I have loved my portion of life,
the singular parts, the plot beneath,
my children with their deep—set eyes,
my friends who seem to understand
what I am all about.

I would not choose to quit the scene,
leave amber lights for an unlit stage,
relinquish passion to the dust.
But old age directs a script
no actor can refuse to play.

Not Everyone's Beach Day

The weather man says,
"The gulf is calm today."
I don't go to the beach
to validate his opinion.
I simply note in my little book
that the gulf is calm & I with it.
Though I am ninty one, it is too soon
to speculate on tides or wind
or when the sun will set.

The Loss Of An Old Friend

Her causes no longer hold
an audience. Her arrogance
is ugly, without compassion
for what she sees of the world
and its inhabitants.
Her spirit stifles in her bones.
Where once her flame
ignited love, indifference denies
the heart's high purpose.

Friendship In Old Age

I'm losing old friends.
Some are slipping into a night of unreachable people.
I no longer go home, to the Cape, that is.
A few old friends come South for the winter.
We phone one another, talk of weather,
our health, the problems of aging.
We make plans to meet for lunch. But then,
we're all too tired to dress & go
beyond our condominium's gates.
And we've heard the stories before,
when we were part of their endings.

Walking in the evening to pick up my mail,
I may meet a stranger there. Another woman.
And we may talk. Excluding the
particulars of pasts we cannot share,
we may begin to fill the space between
her life & mine. And after a while she may
become a new old friend. But then, she too
may pass beyond recall as people do.
After that, I'll have my mail delivered
and maybe get a little dog.

What's Her Name

An old friend is the dessert we eat
after a lifetime of meals.
We only hope that when we meet
we'll be able to remember
what the meals were made of
as we talk across the table.

One More Loss

Giving up life long before she died,
Her talent & passion
Folded into the woman she had become:
A frail remnant of self, nursed by booze,
Shuffling about in a soiled robe,
Complaining, "Life is too boring to live."

That Time Of Year

Dark and humid days
press upon my spirit.
In the lower garden
the last of annuals
blacken in their beds.
Time settles into shade.

Born Again

They say:
Where Eden greens the fruit is large,
flowers swarm & tree frogs sing.
You near a land where dreaming ends,
where you will wake & life begins.

I respond:
I've searched the back room of my mind
where squid-like, shy precognition
dwells in what we've come to believe is
our difference from the animals.

But, with closely related DNA,
how can I know that I am more
than a chimpanzee or an elephant,
or the victim for a hungry cat?

They persist:
If you believe the written Word
you will rise up as Man perfected.
Christ the key to Eden's gate.

Still, I suspect:
There'll come a time when my energy
will pop the cork & dissipate
into the void of mindless space.
Though I might wish it otherwise.

An Easy Way Out

When one settles for a twig
that settles for a flower
that does not insist on the pain of fruit
one's passage is a simple one.

No Futures Contract

Can I in this old age of mine
return to walk a path
where children & I have shared
portions of each other's space?

Or have the years subsequent to
slivers of shared reality
slashed the seams that made a whole
to a pattern too tattered to mend?

In their maturity & my old age
can conversation mitigate
a divergence of need & taste
or the pace at which we walk?

In one's old age will they assist
in the growing need for care
when the years impair to uselessness
one's body or one's intellect?

But after years of swollen feet,
prudence may offer an alternative
to an over-extended peregrination
by inviting Death onto the walk.

Historical Relevance

How can I judge immortality,
in the ecclesiastical sense, that is.
I know I'll die in the short term.
All I have to do is to look around.
Corpses are spread out all over the place.

But this other thing, the question surrounding
the long term, the cosmos beyond the grave,
a god acquitting me of this or that
as he stamps my passport to paradise.

Talking to a Christian I know,
historical relevance
imposes an informed advantage
to her side of the argument.

Still, I usually respond to her belief
in what amounts to cannibalism,
confronting her erudition with,
"Oh yeah? That's what you think."

Who Am I In All Of This?

The past creeps by me.
I try to keep it in its place
not look it in the eye,
forgive it or be forgiven by it.
But incidents without remedy
remain like thorns on a vine
whose bloom has passed.

Old age can't countenance too much truth.
Yet I lift veils from myriad plots
to appraise my part in them,
to acquit or not, to understand a history
elemental to myself. To finally know
who I am in all of this.

Winding through a maze of children,
siblings, parents, lovers, friends,
I search for who I am as part of them.
Wishing to know yet to be free.
Wishing to take but to leave behind
the pain of recognition.

As A Moth Would Do

Is my heart's passion pulsing me
beyond the power of its beat?
Will I, like a moth, fall to flame
or being prudent, blow it out?

Just The Way Things Are

I love the persistence of nature.
Turtles may seize the feet of chicks
as they learn to navigate water.
But there will be one that avoids the fate
of its sisters & its brothers.

I love the random growth of trees
where fire may destroy
the elders in a stand of oak.
But beneath the char, saplings sprout
unimpaired by nature's scorch.

I love that man is optimistic.
That he believes he will survive
his purgatorial span on earth
to arrive at immortality.

I love that death is a cover-up
for those who wrong humanity.
That for coming generations
the narcotic of forgetfulness
will bury the guilty with the slain.

I love it all for sanity's sake.
For moments of beauty that occasion gift,
for compassion, for generosity,
for intellect & meaning.
I love it all for my life's sake.

Ah! Were It But So

I have come to a realization.
My lustful romp is over.
My spirit is a rat deserting a ship.
My lifeline has lost its slack.
Soon the sea will enlist my dust
as dust & water finally mix,
as all of memory swims in schools
bound for a Stygian sleep.

And yet I feel I am as once I was:
Tremulous before a man,
enthralled by a field in late October,
cicadas chomping as golden wreaths
of memorial grass whisper,
"It's not so bad to die. Just look at us!"

If I could have a god the way so many do
and know for sure that he would see me through,
that he would hold me in his arms,
express immortal love, then death
would be exciting, less human,
and I might welcome it!

The Great Power

for Natalie R

Oh! Power beyond my comprehension,
why do you threaten our universe?
What gain for you by losing us
who hold you in such high esteem?

Oh! Power defining every creed
connecting man to man and man to God,
why do you not increase the share
falling to the least of us?

Oh! Power are you so helpless then
against the metamorphosis
that relegates our hapless dreams
to the chaos of perpetual night?

Facing Up

Life grows old
and everyone who uses life
for one thing or another
grows old as well.

All of art & practices.
all of recorded thought
provide no brakes to bring to a stop
life on its way to death.

Unless, of course, one can believe
in a transcendental reality
beyond the life that's lived
irrespective of its quality.

And unless, of course, one can believe
that the messages in DNA
won't interrupt one's mortal chain
to immortality.

Still, life grows old.
Science & learning stop at the gate
where man is alone with his ignorance,
and his will is a passing phase.

The Comfort Of Darkness

I love the privacy of sleep
where nothing more concrete than dreams
pricks my consciousness.
I love the falling back
into my own geometry
whose lines waking cannot articulate.

On The Edge Of Each Cliff

I've stood in a gallery, cool and contained
as marble is cool, as guards are serene,
observing the relics that travel the world
with aplomb I have learned from irrational things.

I've sat out a term in medieval style
reworking a pattern of mille fleur,
a housewife engaged in a newly learned craft
common to women who must manage loss.

I've read the romance in *War and Peace,*
understood Nora, applauded Joan,
was moved by the gleam in Bishop's eye.
And even for a while, I agreed with the French.

I've listened to Mozart, divinely conceived,
with intervals pacing inevitable heights,
easing digestion when heard through a meal,
pleasing to soul & body alike.

I've sat in a bathtub designed by Wright.
Hit my head on a wall bending down for soap.
Forgave him later in the dining room
where tropical birds perched behind glass.

I've lived in a villa in Tuscany,
walked stone beaches in the south of France,
visited England, Spain & Greece,
traveled roads that were painted pink.

I've gambled and lost a fortune or two,
been able to work in the face of it.
I've sung, acted, written, painted.
Like Zelda, I've leaned toward the edge of cliffs.

I've lain with desire, made notes on its fate.
Like a mollusk teased open it trembles in light,
is gulped in one swallow without aftertaste.
I have children I love, friends I admire,
a house at the Cape, the freedom of flight.

What do I miss in my old age?
A world barely skimmed, an art to practice,
and a place to live that I call home.

Possibilities

One good thing about dying
is the possibility of renewal.
Laughter finding jokes that were lost
in the isles of depression,
fresh confrontations with truth & beauty,
passion regaining its edge.

It makes for ease *in extremis*
to believe one will return
to better the battlements of before,
to protect one's heart from ruin.

How impatient I grow just thinking
of a chance to sing another tune,
of not losing fortunes to snake eyes again
but securing them to the moon.

I'd love to live life one more time
magically reincarnated
though not as a bug but as myself
vastly improved by time & space.

To Die By Choice

Fear is a cancer in the conscious mind.
Fear of death but also fear of living.
When insufficiencies outweigh desire
to live beyond prognostication,
one can die with lessened fear
when living becomes what one fears most

Two Together Are Better Than One

My friends and I share joint accounts
in a bank of memories
from which we borrow for small exchanges.
Making appointments to see one another,
we laugh & say, "God willing."
Our little joke against the interest
that accrues and, one day, must be paid.

So—What Else Is New?

I'm feeling wobbly on my feet.
A function of aging, as they say.
And since I do not see so well,
It makes it hard to cross the street
With that conviction I once held
That crossing it, I'd reach the other side.

Carnival Cruise

When I gather up my things
For the Carnival cruise beyond the Atlantic,
I'll take my children's pictures with me
To keep them visible
As I pass from one time zone to another.

NPR

Throughout the day
I listen to the tragedies of our times
on National Public Radio
where abortions of history bleed
creation into the ground,
where all who suffer cry out to be heard.
How to be sanguine listening to
the business news reporting
the latest rape in the slums of greed!
Or atrocities reported by those
who know better than we
how the world turns.

But—in the evening,
I sit on my patio overlooking
a builder's pond in Naples, Florida.
As the moon rises in the east
the sun layers the western sky
in a paling glow of color even as I
reflect upon the day's events, paling too
in the fragile wit of memory.

I have retired here, away from the cold.
I am too old for it. The cold that is.
My children have just telephoned.
Their language is a thread
binding up the evening with precious knots.
Sipping wine from Irish cut glass,
with crackers & a wedge of cheese
handy to my fingertips,
I relish the harmony of sound & light
as I listen to NPR's
classical hour playing Mozart

Retirement

I live around the corner from Death.
I see him on occasion but at a distance
when he visits a neighbor or a friend.

My garden has dwindled over the years.
But today, I planted a rose
which I will feed and tend,
grow optimistic with its bloom.

And live in hope that we, the rose and I,
can grow to blossom one more time
before the cold involves us.